COBBLESTONE · **THE CIVIL WAR**

Ulysses S. Grant
Confident Leader and Hero

Cobblestone Publishing
A Division of Carus Publishing
Peterborough, NH
www.cobblestonepub.com

Staff

Editorial Director: Lou Waryncia

Editor: Meg Chorlian

Book Design: David Nelson, www.dnelsondesign.com

Proofreaders: Meg Chorlian, Sarah Elder Hale, Eileen Terrill

Text Credits

The content of this volume is derived from articles that first appeared in *COBBLESTONE* magazines. Contributing Writers: Roberta Baxter, Craig E. Blohm, Virginia Calkins, Mary Morton Cowan, Lori A. Gordon, Meg Greene, Harold Holzer, Joan Hunt, Loretta Ichord, Kathiann M. Kowalski, Richard K. Munro, John Y. Simon, Glennette Tilley Turner

Picture Credits

Photos.com: 3; Library of Congress: 7, 8, 9, 10, 12, 13, 14, 18, 21 (both), 22, 23, 25, 26, 27, 28, 29, 34, 35, 36, 37, 38, 39, 40, 41, 42; Clipart.com: 5, 6 (inset), 11, 15, 19, 31, 33, 43; Dover Publications: 4; National Archives and Records Administration: 6 (bottom), 20; Fred Carlson: 16–17, 44–45; Jack Williams: 30; Illinois State Historical Library: 32. Images for "Civil War Time Line," pages 44–45, courtesy of Photos.com, Clipart.com, and Library of Congress.

Cover

Ole Peter Hansen Balling, *Grant and His Generals*

National Portrait Gallery, Smithsonian Institution

Library of Congress Cataloging-in-Publication Data

Ulysses S. Grant: confident leader and hero / [project director, Lou Waryncia].

    p. cm. — (Cobblestone the Civil War)

    Includes index.

    ISBN 0-8126-7906-7 (hardcover)

    1. Grant, Ulysses S. (Ulysses Simpson), 1822-1885—Juvenile literature. 2. Generals—United States—Biography—Juvenile literature. 3. United States. Army—Biography—Juvenile literature. 4. United States—History –Civil War, 1861-1865—Juvenile literature. 5. Presidents—United States —Biography—Juvenile literature.

    I. Waryncia, Lou. II. Hale, Sarah Elder. III. Series.

    E672.U385 2005

    973.8'2'092—dc22

    [B]
    2005015827

Printed in China

Cobblestone Publishing

30 Grove Street, Suite C

Peterborough, NH 03458

www.cobblestonepub.com

Table of Contents

A Passion for Horses

Georgetown, Ohio, was full of excitement. A traveling circus was in town. In the ring, a trick pony threw off one rider after another. Then came young Ulysses Grant's turn. The pony bucked and kicked, but Ulysses hung on. A clown tossed a monkey onto the pony's back, but nothing could distract the boy. He clung on and won the prize.

A Shy Boy

Jesse and Hannah Simpson Grant's first child was born on April 27, 1822, in a two-room house overlooking the Ohio River. Named Hiram Ulysses, the boy was called Ulysses.

Throughout his life, Ulysses had a passion for horses. His father, Jesse Grant, owned and operated a successful tannery. As a toddler, Ulysses crawled among the teams of horses at the tannery, sometimes swinging from their tails.

In school, Ulysses solved math problems easily but did not care much for other subjects. No one knew what he did care for, because he was very quiet. A short, stocky boy, Ulysses was not athletic and was painfully shy like his mother, causing townspeople to pick on him. Some folks nicknamed him "Useless."

Shy as he seemed among people, he was confident with horses. By age five, he could stand on the back of a horse while it trotted. Two or three years later, he harnessed and drove teams by himself. At 11, he did all the cultivating and harvesting on the farm and hauled wood for the family and the tannery. Ulysses was so skillful at breaking a feisty colt to saddle or harness that men paid him to break their new horses.

Ulysses did not care for the sights and smells of his father's tannery in Ohio.

Lessons in Bargaining

Once, Ulysses was determined to have a certain horse. His father agreed to pay $25 for it, and he gave his son some bargaining advice. The eight-year-old told the owner, "Papa says I may offer you 20 dollars for the colt, but if you won't take that, I am to offer 22.50, and if you won't take that, I am to give you 25." Ulysses may not have been a respectable horse trader at age eight, but he was undeniably honest. He got what he wanted, too, but he also got what he did not want — wisecracks. Folks teased "Useless" about that horse trade for a long time.

Ulysses preferred activities he could do alone or with a few friends, such as fishing or swimming in the creek. He refused to hunt, for he did not enjoy killing animals. Perhaps that is why he detested his father's tannery. Killing animals and tanning their hides horrified him. The tannery also smelled awful. Whenever his father needed extra help, Ulysses paid schoolmates to work in his place.

Life at West Point

By chance, Jesse Grant learned of an opening for an Ohio man at the U.S. Military Academy in West Point, New York, and he arranged to have his son appointed. Military life did not appeal to Ulysses, and he feared he would fail the entrance exam, but rather than argue with his father, he consented.

When 17-year-old Ulysses arrived at West Point in May 1839, he discovered that he had not been registered under his given name. Unknown to him, his congressman had made an error on his appointment papers, assuming Grant's first name to be Ulysses and his middle name Simpson (his mother's maiden name). Either he was Ulysses S. Grant or he could go home. Having never liked the way his initials spelled "HUG," he accepted his new name. His new initials — "U.S." — sparked another nickname, "Uncle Sam," which was soon shortened to "Sam."

The U.S. Military Academy in West Point, New York, produced a number of officers who later fought against each other in the Civil War.

Ulysses did not like drill practice and could not keep step in the marching band, but mostly he stayed out of trouble. Like every cadet, he received demerits, but his were mostly for minor infractions — perhaps leaving a button undone on his uniform or reporting late for duty. In the history of West Point, only one man had graduated with no demerits — Robert E. Lee.

Next Stop...Missouri

Ulysses was known for his daring horsemanship at West Point and set a school jumping record that stood for years. But he did not set any academic records. His grades in mathematics were excellent, but his other grades pulled his rank down to 21st in a class of 39.

Upon graduation in 1843, Second Lieutenant Ulysses S. Grant requested a cavalry appointment but was instead assigned to the 4th Infantry, stationed in St. Louis, Missouri. He planned to complete his required military service, then teach mathematics. Circumstances beyond his control, however, would change his plans.

Family Man

From poverty to fame and back again, Ulysses S. Grant and his wife, Julia Dent Grant, stood by each other for almost 37 years of marriage. Ulysses met Julia when he was a young lieutenant at Jefferson Barracks, Missouri. The family of his West Point classmate Frederick Dent lived nearby, and Grant began to spend a lot of time at their home, White Haven. Grant learned that he and Frederick's sister, Julia, shared a love for horses, and the two often went riding together.

A Proposal

One day when the couple was traveling to a friend's wedding, they had to cross a rickety bridge over a racing river. Grant promised to protect Julia, and she clung fast to him. When they reached the other side, Grant asked her, "How would you like to cling to me for the rest of your life?"

Julia said yes to the proposal, but the couple had to wait four years until the U.S.–Mexican War (1846–1848) was over before they could marry. Their first son, Frederick Dent, was born on May 30, 1850. They were expecting their second son, Ulysses, Jr. (nicknamed "Buck"), when Grant was transferred by the Army to the West Coast in the summer of 1852.

"You do not know how forsaken I feel here!" he wrote to Julia from Fort Humboldt, California. Desperately missing his wife and children, unable to raise enough money for his family's trip west, and developing a drinking problem, Grant resigned from the Army in April 1854 and returned to White Haven.

Ulysses S. Grant decided to try farming upon his return from California in 1854. He built a home, Hardscrabble, on land in St. Louis, Missouri, that Julia had received as a wedding present.

Grant proved to be an excellent commander during the Civil War, but he remained happiest when his family was with him.

A Difficult Problem

Ulysses S. Grant and his wife, Julia, looked at slavery in very different ways. Julia's family had owned slaves for many years, and she kept slaves even after she married Grant.

In contrast, Grant's father, Jesse, was bitterly opposed to slavery. Jesse had once worked at a tannery owned by Owen Brown, whose son John later led the famous raid at Harpers Ferry, Virginia, in 1859. Although Jesse and his wife, Hannah, said that they would not fit in at the elegant Dent home, one of the reasons they did not attend their son's wedding was probably because the Dent family owned slaves.

Grant did not publicly challenge the Dents' position on slavery. While struggling as a poor farmer in 1859, however, he freed William Jones, a slave given to him by Julia's father. And in 1862, when his wife's slave, Black Julia, ran away in Mississippi, he refused to pursue her.

Constant Struggle

Civilian life was a constant struggle for Grant. He worked hard but had bad luck as a farmer. He also was unable to support his family with a job in real estate. Unemployed, he turned to his father for help. He became the accountant for his father's leather business in Galena, Illinois, at a salary of $600 a year.

Despite their financial problems, the Grants were happy. In 1855, their daughter, Ellen (nicknamed "Nellie"), was born. Their fourth child, Jesse, arrived in 1858. Grant loved spending time with his children.

Back in the Army

When the Civil War broke out in 1861, Grant rejoined the Army. He was commissioned a colonel of the 21st Illinois Volunteers. Once again, he was separated from his family. He wrote home often, sending Julia love and "kisses for you and the children."

Whenever possible, his family visited him at camp. Over the years, Julia and some or all of the children joined him in Cairo, Illinois; Corinth, Mississippi; and at least a dozen other places.

Fast Fact

The U.S.–Mexican War (1846–1848) resulted in Mexico giving up

2/5

of its territory to the United States.

A family man to the end, Grant is surrounded by his wife, children, and grandchildren shortly before his death.

The children loved visiting their father at army camp. "To the small boy it was 'father's army,'" recalled his youngest son, Jesse. Often the soldiers would carve toys or make molasses candy over the campfire. Jesse especially loved riding with his father to inspect the troops, either mounted on his own Shetland pony or perched behind his father on a big buckskin horse named Mankiller.

A Compassionate Leader

Grant's love for his family made him sensitive to the families of all soldiers. After victory in battle, he acted compassionately, seeing that everyone got food and medical attention. "This will all come out right in good time," he once assured Julia, "and you must not forget that each and every one of my soldiers has a mother, wife, or sweetheart, whose lives are as dear to them as mine is to you."

Rising Through the Ranks

When the Civil War began, 38-year-old Ulysses S. Grant's fortunes had fallen so far that the veteran could not even get himself assigned to a small command. By the time the war was over, though, he was the most celebrated military hero in the nation. No American officer ever rose higher or faster than Grant.

Earning Respect

Not until a sympathetic Illinois governor came to his aid in the spring of 1861 did the frustrated Grant win appointment as a colonel of the 21st

The Union army's successful attack of Fort Donelson drew the attention of President Abraham Lincoln, who promptly promoted Ulysses S. Grant to major general.

Illinois Volunteer Infantry. Within two months, he had transformed a group of unruly, inexperienced men into a polished fighting force and was promoted to brigadier general.

Grant's path to glory was not smooth. His first battle as a commander — an attack on a Confederate camp in Belmont, Missouri, in November 1861 — ended without significant success. Grant lost more than one-fifth of his men. But his aggressiveness in the field won the attention of his superiors, who were frustrated by the caution so many other Union generals were showing at the time. He also earned the respect of his men by the calm way in which he organized the Union retreat.

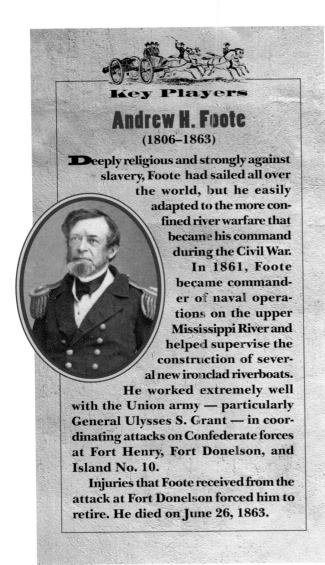

Valuable Victories

Grant came into his own in February 1862, when he captured two crucial Confederate river strongholds, Fort Henry and Fort Donelson in Tennessee. Fort Henry was the first major Union victory of the Civil War. Working in cooperation with the Union navy under Commodore Andrew H. Foote, Grant took the Tennessee River fortification on February 6, 1862.

Next, Grant marched 12 miles to Fort Donelson. Located on the Cumberland River, Fort Donelson guarded the approach to Nashville. Although initially repelled by the Confederates, Grant successfully took the fort after several days of bombardment by land and sea. From these points, the Union army was able to continue its progress to the Mississippi River, eventually controlling the major interior waterways all the way to Louisiana.

'Unconditional Surrender'

In the midst of his ferocious attack on Fort Donelson, its commander, Confederate general Simon Bolivar Buckner, sent Grant a message asking his terms for a cease-fire.

Grant quickly replied that he would accept nothing less than "unconditional and immediate surrender." These words coincided with his initials. In the North, U.S. Grant became known to an adoring public as "Unconditional Surrender" Grant. President Abraham Lincoln immediately promoted him to major general of volunteers. Two months later, Grant would be involved in one of the war's bloodiest and brutal clashes at Shiloh, Tennessee.

Underestimating the Enemy at Shiloh

A surprise attack by the Confederates and then an unexpected counterattack by the Union troops the next day made Shiloh the scene of a shockingly bloody battle.

While Major General Ulysses S. Grant ate breakfast on April 6, 1862, he heard the roar of cannon seven miles away. He suddenly realized that he had made a terrible mistake. A great battle had begun!

Grant had brought his army up the Tennessee River to attack Confederate forces at Corinth, Mississippi. But while Grant prepared his army and waited for Major General Don Carlos

Buell and his 20,000 troops to arrive, the Confederates had unexpectedly attacked the Union army encamped at Shiloh. Some of Grant's troops were still asleep when the Confederates charged at five in the morning. Many Union soldiers fled in panic.

Checking the Panic

Grant boarded a steamboat to join his army. He ordered reinforcements to assemble at Pittsburg Landing, a steamboat docking site on the Tennessee River and the gathering point for his army. When Grant reached the battlefield, he found that his army had been forced back. There was danger of the Confederate army trapping the Union forces against the swollen Tennessee River. Already many soldiers huddled in panic at the riverbank, hoping to be evacuated.

The timely arrival of Major General Don Carlos Buell and his army in the evening of April 6 provided Grant with the manpower to counterattack on April 7.

Fortunately for Grant, steadfast troops under Brigadier General Benjamin M. Prentiss delayed the Confederate advance until late afternoon. After hours of fighting, Prentiss and his men became isolated and surrounded, and they surrendered. But they had given the rest of the Union army time to form a line of defense along the bluff overlooking the river. After dark, Buell's reinforcements arrived. Grant's army had been mauled that day, but he was already thinking about how he would whip the enemy the next day.

Hammering Away

Grant attacked the next morning. This time, the Confederates were surprised. They had been so successful the day before that they had expected to win easily on the second day of the battle. The Confederate commander, Albert Sidney Johnston, had been killed during the first day of fighting, and his replacement, General Pierre G.T. Beauregard, now had fewer men than Grant's reinforced army. Grant hammered the Confederates with all his troops. After a second day of hard fighting, Beauregard withdrew toward Corinth.

The Union army was left in possession of the battlefield and could claim a bloody victory. Casualties on both sides were enormous: The North had lost more than 13,000 men, the South more than 10,000. No previous battle fought in the United States had left so many dead and wounded.

Northern Critics

Grant's army had been on the verge of defeat after an initial day of bloody fighting at Shiloh. But he had refused to retreat and with bulldog determination rallied his troops to triumph by attacking ferociously the next morning. Some critics labeled Grant a butcher, a charge that would hound him for the rest of the war. Other critics whispered that Grant drank too much.

Pierre G.T. Beauregard had earned the nickname "Little Napoleon" while at West Point for his interest in that French general.

> ## "I can't spare this man: he fights."
> — **Abraham Lincoln**

After the battle, some Northern newspapers criticized Grant for not preparing for the Confederate attack. They blamed him for the many casualties and called for his removal. President Abraham Lincoln, however, admired Grant for his attack on the second day. Lincoln knew that generals afraid to fight battles would never win the war. He decided that Grant was a fighting general and insisted, "I can't spare this man: he fights."

Keeping Cool

At Shiloh, Grant showed what kind of general he was. He kept cool in the midst of battle. As he rallied his men to avoid defeat on the first day of fighting, he planned his strategy for a successful counterattack. His calm self-confidence encouraged teenage boys to fight like veterans.

Grant learned valuable lessons in each battle. The Battle of Shiloh taught him not to underestimate the enemy. Two years later, by the time he began the final campaign against Confederate general Robert E. Lee, Grant had mastered the strategy that eventually brought an end to the war.

Fast Fact

The Battle of Shiloh earned its name from a small local church named Shiloh, which means "place of peace."

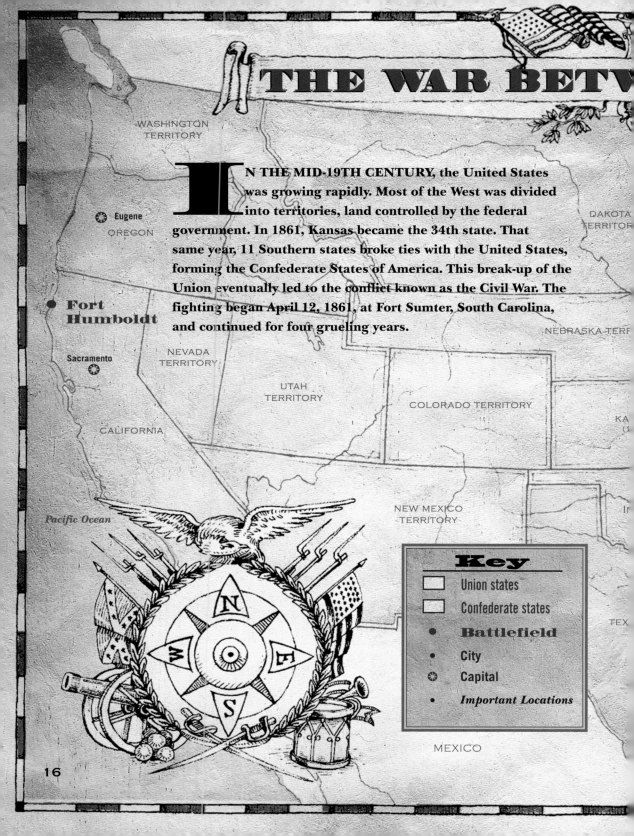

WASHINGTON
TERRITORY

Eugene
OREGON

DAKOTA
TERRITOR

IN THE MID-19TH CENTURY, the United States was growing rapidly. Most of the West was divided into territories, land controlled by the federal government. In 1861, Kansas became the 34th state. That same year, 11 Southern states broke ties with the United States, forming the Confederate States of America. This break-up of the Union eventually led to the conflict known as the Civil War. The fighting began April 12, 1861, at Fort Sumter, South Carolina, and continued for four grueling years.

NEBRASKA TERF

● Fort
Humboldt

NEVADA
TERRITORY

Sacramento

UTAH
TERRITORY

COLORADO TERRITORY

KA
(1

CALIFORNIA

Pacific Ocean

NEW MEXICO
TERRITORY

Ir

Key

☐ Union states

☐ Confederate states

● **Battlefield**

• City

◉ Capital

• *Important Locations*

TEX

MEXICO

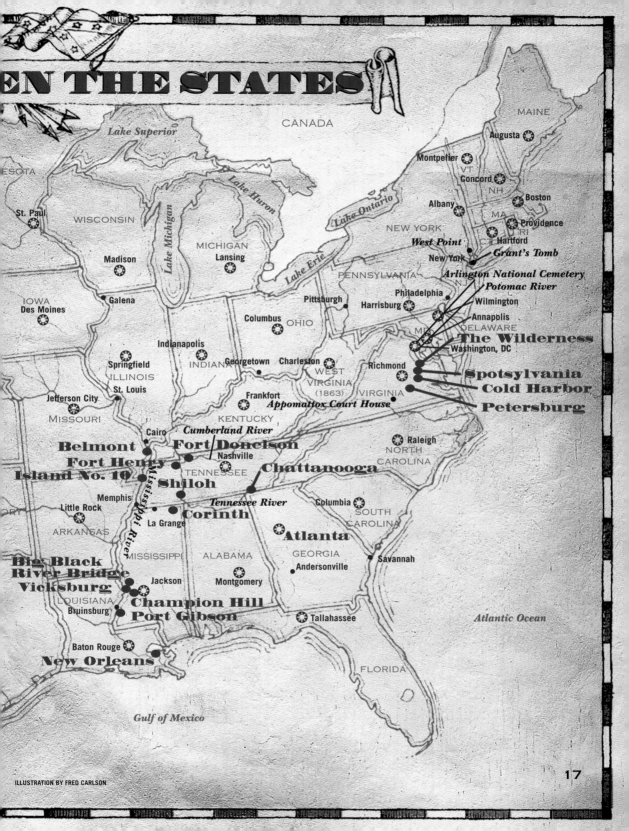

CANADA

MAINE

Lake Superior

Augusta

Montpelier

Concord

VT

NH

ESOTA

Lake Huron

Lake Ontario

Albany

Boston

St. Paul

WISCONSIN

Lake Michigan

MICHIGAN

Lansing

NEW YORK

Hartford

Providence

RI

West Point

Madison

Lake Erie

PENNSYLVANIA

New York

Grant's Tomb

IOWA

Des Moines

Galena

Pittsburgh

Philadelphia

Harrisburg

Arlington National Cemetery

NJ

Potomac River

Wilmington

Columbus

OHIO

DELAWARE

Annapolis

MD

Indianapolis

Charleston

Richmond

The Wilderness

Washington, DC

Springfield

ILLINOIS

INDIANA

Georgetown

WEST

VIRGINIA

(1863)

VIRGINIA

Spotsylvania

Cold Harbor

St. Louis

Jefferson City

Frankfort

Appomattox Court House

Petersburg

MISSOURI

KENTUCKY

Cairo

Cumberland River

Fort Donelson

Nashville

Raleigh

NORTH

CAROLINA

Belmont

Fort Henry

Island No. 10

Mississippi River

Shiloh

TENNESSEE

Chattanooga

Memphis

Tennessee River

Columbia

Little Rock

La Grange

Corinth

SOUTH

CAROLINA

ARKANSAS

MISSISSIPPI

ALABAMA

Atlanta

GEORGIA

ORY

Savannah

Big Black

River Bridge

Vicksburg

Jackson

Andersonville

Montgomery

LOUISIANA

Bruinsburg

Champion Hill

Port Gibson

Tallahassee

Atlantic Ocean

Baton Rouge

New Orleans

FLORIDA

Gulf of Mexico

By Land, By Sea, and By...Horse?

In the spring of 1863, Union major general Ulysses S. Grant had command of 60,000 men in the Army of the Tennessee. He had been given a free hand by his superior officer, General Henry W. Halleck, to pick his own fights. Grant had picked Vicksburg. The Union army, however, had many miles to travel and many battles to fight before it would even reach that Confederate stronghold.

Distracting the Enemy

Grant knew that the fate of Vicksburg would determine the fate of the Confederacy. In March 1863, he began a new offensive that he hoped would finally bring success. He decided to move his army down the

Once safely past the Confederate blockade at Vicksburg, the Union navy provided transport and supplies for Grant's final campaign against the fortified city in 1863.

west side of the Mississippi River in Louisiana. They then would cross the river south of Vicksburg and march north to the weaker southern flank of the city. But first Grant wanted to distract the Confederates. He ordered other troop movements to confuse them.

Major General William T. Sherman was directed to keep up the pressure north of the city. In December 1862, Sherman had attempted to attack Vicksburg on its northern side. The city's elaborate defense works proved far too strong. Sherman's continued northern presence and periodic attacks, however, kept the Confederates focused there and not on Grant's movements across the river to the south.

Meanwhile, on the night of April 16–17, Rear Admiral David Dixon Porter sailed his 11-vessel Union fleet south past the intense bombardment of Vicksburg's roaring cannon. He lost only one ship. His role in the Vicksburg campaign was to carry supplies to Grant once he arrived south of Vicksburg and to transport the Union soldiers across the river to the eastern shore.

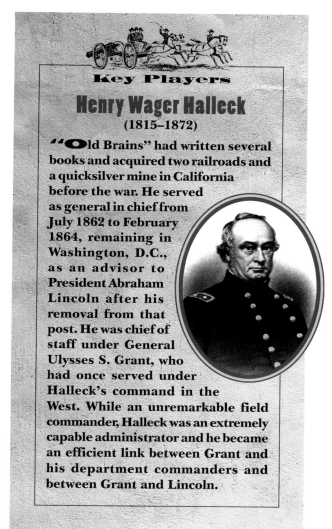

Key Players

Henry Wager Halleck
(1815–1872)

"Old Brains" had written several books and acquired two railroads and a quicksilver mine in California before the war. He served as general in chief from July 1862 to February 1864, remaining in Washington, D.C., as an advisor to President Abraham Lincoln after his removal from that post. He was chief of staff under General Ulysses S. Grant, who had once served under Halleck's command in the West. While an unremarkable field commander, Halleck was an extremely capable administrator and he became an efficient link between Grant and his department commanders and between Grant and Lincoln.

A Daring Cavalry Raid

Simultaneously, on April 17, a cavalry raid from La Grange, Tennessee, to Baton Rouge, Louisiana, was launched. Grant wanted to confuse the Confederates concerning his true intentions. The commander in charge of the raid was Colonel Benjamin H. Grierson.

Trying to stop Grierson's attacking troops were large numbers of Confederates. But to trick them, Grierson split his forces. He sent 700 men north while the main body — 1,000 strong — continued south. He directed the destruction of key portions of the Southern

Railroad, which led to Jackson and Vicksburg from the east, and the Mississippi Central Railroad, which was 30 miles south of Jackson. Like Grant, Grierson wanted to confuse the Confederates. He used Union soldiers dressed in gray (the Confederate color) to send a false telegraph message to Vicksburg regarding his whereabouts.

On April 27, General John C. Pemberton, Confederate commander in Vicksburg, ordered Colonel Wirt Adams's cavalry to leave western Mississippi and go after Grierson. The result was that Grant's landing was almost unopposed. By April 30, Porter was ferrying Grant's troops to the east bank of the Mississippi River at Bruinsburg.

Moving Inland

Grant was now on the same side of the river as Vicksburg, just below the city. Moving inland, he captured Port Gibson on May 1. On May 2, after a 16-day campaign, Grierson's weary troops entered Union-held Baton Rouge. His men had made a more than 600-mile ride through the heart of the Confederacy. Sherman called it "the most brilliant expedition of the war." Grierson had lost only a few men, but had managed to destroy railroads, telegraph lines, arms, and Confederate government supplies.

The risk of splitting up his army paid off for Grant. He arrived outside Vicksburg on May 18 after winning each battle with the Confederate troops who had been sent to stop him. But the city itself was fortified and Grant's work was not yet done. He would be forced to settle in for a siege.

Key Players
David Dixon Porter
(1813–1891)

When the Civil War began, Porter had already served many years in the U.S. Navy — having begun his naval career before he was a teenager. He helped plan the attack on New Orleans, Louisiana, in 1862 and was in command of a squadron during the fight. Named as commander of the Mississippi River Squadron a year later, Porter cooperated with Union army commander Ulysses S. Grant to capture the important Confederate city of Vicksburg.

In January 1865, Porter's ships began bombarding the strongest fort left in the Confederacy: Fort Fisher at the mouth of the Cape Fear River, near Wilmington, North Carolina. It fell the following month. After the war, Porter became an admiral and was the highest-ranking U.S. naval officer for the next 21 years.

Key Players
Benjamin H. Grierson
(1826–1911)

A former music teacher, Grierson had been kicked in the head by a pony when he was eight years old and lost his sight for two months. Quite naturally, he feared and avoided horses for most of his adult life. He was a strong supporter of President Abraham Lincoln, however, so the crisis of the Civil War led the mild-mannered musician to enlist in 1861 as an infantry private in the Union army.

To his dismay, Grierson was assigned to the 6th Illinois Volunteer Cavalry. His love of country and strong sense of duty helped him conquer his fear of horses. By 1863, he was one of Major General Ulysses S. Grant's top cavalry commanders. His distracting ride during the Vicksburg Campaign proved to be one of the most remarkable cavalry raids of the Civil War. After the Civil War, Grierson led one of the first two regiments of African American soldiers in the U.S. Army.

Major General Ulysses S. Grant's Union forces slowly cut off all avenues of retreat for the defenders of Vicksburg and proceeded to besiege the city for six weeks.

Vicksburg Under Siege

Despite little previous success, Major General Ulysses S. Grant remained determined to capture Vicksburg in the spring of 1863. Union troops had tried digging a canal across the U-shaped turn of the Mississippi River near Vicksburg. This would allow boats to bypass Confederate artillery fire from the high bluffs on which the city was built. It was wet, tiring work that was soon abandoned. Grant next had tried to approach Vicksburg from the north over the swampy bayous, but this plan also had failed.

'Incur No More Losses'

By this time, Confederate troops had retreated into Vicksburg after suffering defeats at Champion Hill and Big Black River Bridge.

"I shall never forget that woeful sight of a beaten, demoralized [discouraged] army that came rushing back — humanity in the last throes of endurance," wrote Dora Miller, a resident of Vicksburg. Grant twice tried to storm the city's defenses on May 19 and May 22, but both attempts failed. "I now determined upon a regular siege, to 'outcamp the enemy,' as it were, and to incur no more losses," Grant later wrote.

Defenses Ready

The Confederates, led by General John C. Pemberton, were ready to defend their city. They had constructed a line of defensive earthworks

If at First You Don't Succeed...

On December 9, 1862, Major General Ulysses S. Grant sent Major General William T. Sherman to Memphis, Tennessee. Sherman commanded four divisions of troops — approximately 33,000 men. Once there, Sherman's troops met with naval forces. Together, they proceeded down the Mississippi River. They landed just north of Vicksburg on December 26.

Sherman's men struggled through swamps and streams to a position near Chickasaw Bayou, Mississippi. They made several unsuccessful attempts to get around the Confederates. On December 29, he ordered a direct attack. The Confederates held strong. With heavy Union casualties, Sherman admitted defeat and withdrew. This Confederate victory in 1862 frustrated Grant's early attempts to take Vicksburg. It made him realize that the city could not be won by attacking from the north.

nine miles long around Vicksburg. The Confederate artillery and infantry could fire down on the enemy with great safety. Union forces soon began digging trenches, or saps, of their own. These saps zigzagged toward the Confederate line and in some places came within 10 or 20 yards of Rebel fortifications.

Grant immediately began a round-the-clock artillery assault against the Confederate line. At the same time, Union gunboats commanded by Rear Admiral David Dixon Porter on the Mississippi River added their own mortar fire.

Emma Balfour, wife of a Vicksburg doctor, described the experience in her diary: "All day and all night the shells from the mortars are falling all around us…. No rest for our poor soldiers who have to stay down in the trenches all day in the hot sun. It is a most discouraging sort of warfare."

Fast Fact

Vicksburg surrendered on July 4, 1863, just **one day** after the famous Battle of Gettysburg.

Digging Caves and Tunnels

Homes and other buildings in the city became dangerous places: "Yesterday morning," Balfour wrote, "a piece of mortar shell struck the schoolroom roof, tore through the partition wall.... Mrs. Hawkes' home is literally torn to pieces...."

To escape the bombardment, many of Vicksburg's citizens dug caves in the hillsides of the city. According to Mary Ann Loughborough, wife of a Confederate soldier, "In the evening we were terrified...by the loud rush and scream of mortar shells; we ran to the small cave near the house, and were in it during the night...."

Some caves were used only for safety during bombardment, while housekeeping was set up in larger caves for the duration of the siege. Furniture, lamps, beds, and other items needed for life underground were brought in. Rugs covered the walls to combat dampness.

While Vicksburg's residents were digging caves, Grant's troops were doing some digging of their own. Soldiers began tunneling toward a Confederate fortification manned by the 3rd Louisiana Infantry. By mid-June, the tunnel had reached nearly 50 feet under the fortification. Union soldiers then packed 2,200 pounds of gunpowder at the end of the tunnel. On June 25, the explosives were detonated. "So terrible a spectacle is seldom witnessed," wrote a newspaper correspondent. "Dust, dirt...timber, gun carriages, logs –– in fact, everything connected with the fort — rose hundreds of feet in the air." Yet despite the spectacular blast, Union troops could not capture the city.

Mule Meat and Boiled Rat

Food in Vicksburg became scarce. Miller wrote, "Rice and milk is my main food; I can't eat the mule meat. We boil the rice and eat it cold with milk for supper." Mule meat may not have appealed to her, but it, along with boiled rat, had become a staple of the Confederate soldiers' diet.

> "All day and all night the shells from the mortars are falling all around us.... It is a most discouraging sort of warfare."
>
> — Emma Balfour

Fast Fact

Control of the Mississippi River made Mississippi an important state. By the end of the Civil War in April 1865, more than

770

battles or skirmishes had taken place there.

Ammunition also ran low. The city of Vicksburg began to show the effects of the siege. Confederate sergeant Willie Tunnard wrote of many "…houses dilapidated and in ruins, rent and torn by shot and shell…. The stores, the few that were open, looked like the ghost of more prosperous times, with their empty shelves and scant stock of goods."

Union forces attempted to blow up the fortifications at Vicksburg, but they were unable to capture the city.

Weary Defenders

By July 3, Pemberton finally admitted that his troops and the city could hold out no longer. He sent a note to Grant asking for terms of surrender. On July 4, 1863, the weary defenders of Vicksburg filed out of the city and laid down their arms. But there was no celebration by Union troops. They stood in silence, showing respect for their worthy adversaries. When President Abraham Lincoln heard of Vicksburg's surrender, he said, "The Father of Waters again goes unvexed to the sea."

After 47 days of siege, Vicksburg had fallen. Combined with the Union victory at Gettysburg the previous day, it was the beginning of the end for the Confederacy.

STEVENS SCHOOL

The Grants' oldest son, Frederick (seated, to the left of Grant, who is standing wearing a hat), was a frequent companion of his father during the Civil War.

'Three Cheers for Young Grant!'

Major General Ulysses S. Grant and his son watched from the gunboat *Henry Von Ahul* as the Union fleet steamed down the Mississippi River past Confederate batteries. Twelve-year-old Fred (he would turn 13 on May 30, 1863) had begged to be allowed to accompany his father on the Vicksburg Campaign. He was very excited.

Pitching In

Leaving Fred asleep on the boat, Grant went ashore the next morning to join his troops. When Fred woke up and realized his father was gone, he jumped ashore. Hoping to find his father, he joined a regiment marching to the front.

Instead, he found himself in the midst of the Battle of Port Gibson (May 1, 1863), which was one of several smaller battles that occurred as part of the larger Vicksburg Campaign. When the fighting ended, Fred pitched in to help bury the dead and take the wounded to a house that was serving as a hospital. Exhausted, he finally fell asleep on the ground, where his amazed father later found him.

Mistaken Identity

Other battles soon followed. In the confusion after the Battle of Champion Hill, when the Union army tried to cut off a Confederate command from retreating to Vicksburg, a party of Union soldiers mistakenly tried to take Fred away as a prisoner. Luckily, an old soldier recognized the boy and yelled, "Three cheers for young Grant!" The red-faced soldiers released Fred and shouted heartily.

Major General Ulysses S. Grant set up his headquarters near Vicksburg on the banks of the Mississippi River.

Once, as Fred watched retreating Confederates swim across the Big Black River, he was hit in the leg by an enemy sharpshooter. "I am killed," Fred told the Union officer who rushed to his aid. When instructed to wiggle his toes, the boy obeyed and realized that the wound, while painful, was not serious.

A City Surrenders

During the siege of Vicksburg, Fred rested in his father's tent. There, on the evening of July 3, a messenger brought a note to Grant. Grant read it, then quietly told Fred, "Vicksburg has surrendered." A jubilant Fred rushed out to spread the good news to the troops.

Grant Takes Command

Lieutenant General Ulysses S. Grant took full command of all Union forces in March 1864 and proved worthy of President Abraham Lincoln's confidence.

Union successes at Shiloh and Vicksburg came at the cost of many lives and after much time was invested. Nevertheless, Grant continued his dogged and aggressive drive on Confederate strongholds. In November 1863,

Grant proceeded to win impressive victories at the battles of Lookout Mountain and Missionary Ridge. By pushing the Confederate armies back from these strategic locations overlooking Chattanooga, Grant was able to break the siege of that city in Tennessee. Grant now was universally recognized as the most successful — and the most feared — Union general. President Abraham Lincoln promoted him to general in chief of all Union armies in March 1864 and awarded him the rank of lieutenant general.

Results, Not Excuses

Grant possessed all of the qualities that Lincoln wanted in an army commander. He fought aggressively, took responsibility for his actions, and avoided politics. Instead of excuses, Grant gave him results. "It is the dogged pertinacity [extreme stubbornness] of Grant that wins," Lincoln said. He trusted his commander in chief on the battlefield, while Grant respected Lincoln's ability to run the nation. It was a winning combination.

Grant's fierce attack not only shattered the Confederate army besieging Chattanooga and freed the Union troops that had bottled up inside the city, but it also opened the South to invasion by the North.

The Wilderness
May 5-6, 1864

APRIL 9, 1865 ~
Surrender at
Appomattox

Siege of
Petersburg
June 20, 1864 ~
April 2, 1865

Chattanooga
Nov. 23-25, 1863

Chickamauga
Sept. 19-20, 1863

Fort
Henry
Feb. 6, 1862

Fort
Donelson
Feb. 16, 1862

Shiloh
April 6-7, 1862

Vicksburg
July 4, 1863

GEN. GRANT'S
MAJOR
CIVIL WAR
BATTLES

Grant took personal command of fighting in the East, while masterminding a coordinated plan to fight the war on other fronts. It was Grant, for example, who helped design and then ordered Major General William T. Sherman's attack on Atlanta in July 1864 and later the famous march through Georgia, which split the Confederacy.

By the end of 1864, Grant was so admired that he probably could have seized the Republican presidential nomination from Lincoln himself. But he refused suggestions that he run for the office, preferring instead to win the war in the field. "I propose to fight it out on this line," he declared, "if it takes all summer."

Pushing South

It did — and more. For the first time, the Union's Army of the Potomac, under Grant's leadership, continued south instead of

Fast Fact

Grant was promoted to full general in 1866, making him the

1st

U.S. citizen after George Washington to hold that rank.

retreating north after each battle. In battle after bloody battle, at places like the Wilderness (May 1864), Spotsylvania (May 1864), and Cold Harbor (June 1864), the Union lost tens of thousands of men to the Army of Northern Virginia, led by General Robert E. Lee. But Grant's forces outnumbered Lee's, and he could replace wounded or killed soldiers more easily. It became a war of attrition; that is, the army that had the greater number of soldiers would win. Slowly but surely, Grant forced the Confederate army to be stretched dangerously thin.

Surrender!

In the spring of 1865, Grant took the city of Petersburg, Virginia, which had been besieged for nearly a year, and then captured Richmond, the capital of the Confederacy. In the final campaign of the war, Grant outmaneuvered Lee and forced him to surrender at Appomattox Court House, Virginia, on April 9, 1865.

On that day, Lee arrived in brilliant dress uniform, a gleaming sword at his side. Grant met him in what Lee described as a "rough traveling suit, the uniform of a private with the straps of a lieutenant-general." The contrast between the two great figures of the war could not have been more dramatic. Grant, who had failed so often before the war, had become one of the most famous Americans of his time.

Even Lee's admirers appreciated that Grant allowed the defeated Confederates to return home to their farms with the horses they had used in battle. Ulysses S. Grant proved as generous in victory as he had been ferocious in battle.

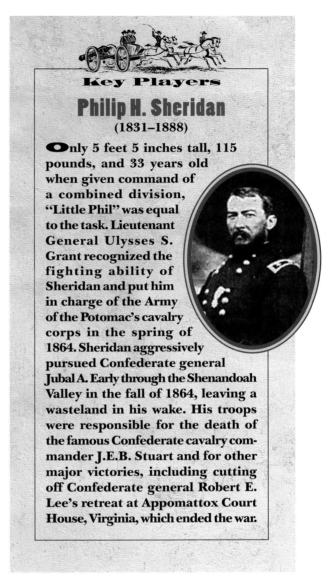

Key Players

Philip H. Sheridan
(1831–1888)

Only 5 feet 5 inches tall, 115 pounds, and 33 years old when given command of a combined division, "Little Phil" was equal to the task. Lieutenant General Ulysses S. Grant recognized the fighting ability of Sheridan and put him in charge of the Army of the Potomac's cavalry corps in the spring of 1864. Sheridan aggressively pursued Confederate general Jubal A. Early through the Shenandoah Valley in the fall of 1864, leaving a wasteland in his wake. His troops were responsible for the death of the famous Confederate cavalry commander J.E.B. Stuart and for other major victories, including cutting off Confederate general Robert E. Lee's retreat at Appomattox Court House, Virginia, which ended the war.

Ely S. Parker, Seneca Chief

In Major General Ulysses S. Grant's recommendation to extend a commission to Seneca chief Ely S. Parker, he praised Parker as a highly educated "full blooded Indian" and an engineer of "considerable eminence."

Ely S. Parker

Parker received notice of his appointment as assistant adjutant general with the rank of captain at Tonawanda Indian Reservation, New York. With the Senecas' blessing, Parker accepted the commission. He joined General John E. Smith's division at Vicksburg, Mississippi, in 1863 and renewed his friendship with Grant, whose army had just captured Vicksburg. Parker had met Grant in 1860 in Galena, Illinois, while working as an engineer there.

Glowing Accounts

Parker's duties as adjutant general included handling correspondence and keeping records. His mastery of the English language served him well in this capacity. His legal and engineering training also benefited the army. In September 1863, he was assigned to Grant's personal military staff. Parker's glowing account of Grant's bravery,

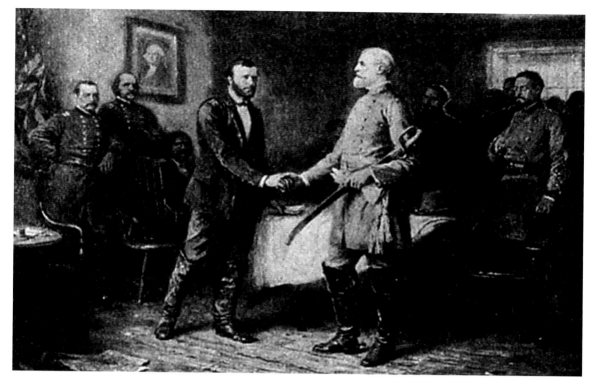

stamina, and military economy during the Battle of Chattanooga, Tennessee, was published in several Northern newspapers.

Terms of Surrender

In August 1864, Parker was appointed Grant's military secretary with the rank of lieutenant colonel. Until the end of the war, Parker wrote Grant's orders and maintained his papers. Perhaps the most important paper he copied for Grant was the terms of surrender presented to General Robert E. Lee at Appomattox Court House, Virginia, on April 9, 1865. After Grant and Lee agreed to the terms of surrender, Parker wrote the official copy of Grant's letter in ink in his fine handwriting. Grant and Lee then signed the document.

Two accounts of the surrender at Appomattox note that when Grant introduced Parker, Lee hesitated before shaking his hand. When Lee realized that Parker was an American Indian, he extended his hand and, according to Parker, said, "I am glad to see one real American here." Parker then shook Lee's hand and replied, "We are all Americans."

Lee's Surrender at Appomattox captures the meeting between generals Ulysses S. Grant and Robert E. Lee in the McLean parlor at Appomattox Court House, Virginia. Parker is shown in the painting to the left of Grant.

National Hero

After the end of the Civil War, Ulysses S. Grant began a new career — as national hero. Crowds gathered to see "the gallant hero who symbolized the valiant struggle to maintain the Union." Individuals, towns, and cities showered him with gifts. He received lavishly furnished homes in Philadelphia, Pennsylvania, and Galena, Illinois; cash in New York City; a collection of leather-bound, gilt-edged books in Boston; and more. It was quite a change for a man who had been largely unknown before the war.

Reconstruction

Eventually, Grant purchased a house in Washington, D.C., and settled in with his family. In 1866, he was promoted to four-star general — the first ever in the U.S. Army. His task was to oversee Reconstruction in the South, when the federal government maintained control of the Southern states as the nation tried to rebuild itself.

The political climate in Washington was unsettled at this time. When President Abraham Lincoln was assassinated in April 1865, Andrew

Johnson had become president. A fierce battle over Reconstruction raged between Johnson and the Radical Republicans in Congress. The Republicans felt that Johnson was too lenient, too ready to forgive and forget.

'Let Us Have Peace'

Grant was drawn into the battle. He served briefly as acting secretary of war under Johnson but found himself more and more in agreement with the Radicals. In 1868, Grant became the Republican presidential candidate because he feared "the loss…of the results of the costly war…we have gone through" and felt he could prevent that from happening. He was not exactly enthusiastic, later saying, "I was forced into it in spite of myself," and did not campaign. But his immense popularity brought victory in 1868 and again in 1872.

A reluctant Grant became involved in politics and agreed to run for president in 1868.

Not everyone was pleased. Former secretary of the Navy Gideon Welles said, "It pained me to see how little he understood of the fundamental principles and structure of our government." But Grant saw the job as a "gift of the people," and his agenda was simple: "A purely administrative officer should always…execute the will of the people…. Let us have peace."

It was a hard time to be president. Relations with Great Britain were strained due to its support of the South during the Civil War. A bloody revolution was under way in Cuba. At home, the nation was still divided. Grant had his work cut out for him.

Scandal and Panic

Throughout both of his terms, Grant's presidency was mired in scandal after scandal. An attempt by Jay Gould and Jim Fisk

PUCK.

(financiers and friends of Grant) to corner the gold market resulted in a stock market crash on Friday, September 24, 1869. Banks failed, stock brokerages closed, and the country panicked.

Grant ended the crisis by releasing government gold reserves, but the scandal of "Black Friday" lingered. Grant's vice president and some members of Congress were entangled in the Crédit Mobilier scandal, which involved insider dealing and bribery during the construction of the Union Pacific Railroad.

Though innocent of any wrongdoing, Grant was guilty of misjudgment. He was a man of honor and loyalty, unable or unwilling to see dishonor and disloyalty in those he trusted. The savvy military leader seemed a poor judge of character in civilian life.

A Nation Begins to Heal

For some Americans, Grant's two-term presidency was quite enough. This editorial cartoon, in which Grant on a trapeze is weighed down by various forms of corruption, wonders about the benefits of a possible third term for the president.

Grant did have some successes. His secretary of state, Hamilton Fish, was an able foreign policy advisor. Advances were made in the more humane treatment of Indians. Taxes were reduced. Grant made gold the money standard, promising that all U.S. debts would be paid back in gold. This helped to curb inflation and stabilize the economy. All of the Southern states were readmitted to the Union, and territorial disputes in the Northwest were settled. The healing of the nation began.

Personally, the Grants were happy in the White House. They

traveled and entertained. After two terms, however, Grant was voted out of office. In December 1876, he addressed Congress: "It was my fortune, or misfortune, to be called to the office of Chief Executive without any previous training…. I have acted…from a conscientious desire to do what was right…and for the…best interests of the…people…. Failures have been errors of judgment, not…intent." In the end, Grant left office "amid general goodwill."

On a World Tour

Civilians again, the Grants decided to travel until their money ran out. In May 1877, they departed for England, where Grant was greeted as a hero. Their world tour lasted more than two years. They met many world leaders, including Queen Victoria and Prime Minister Benjamin Disraeli of England, Otto von Bismarck of Germany, and General Li Hung Chang of China.

When the Grants returned to the United States, Americans greeted their former president with affection, his past "sins" apparently forgiven. There was a suggestion of a third presidential term in 1880, but that effort failed. It was time for Grant to look ahead.

'To Witness These Things'

On a summer day in 1884, Ulysses S. Grant sat down to lunch at his vacation home in Long Branch, New Jersey. While eating a peach, he complained of a terrible pain in his throat.

At first, he shrugged it off. But the pain was more than a minor annoyance. When he returned to New York City in the fall, Grant visited a local specialist. The diagnosis was not good. Grant was suffering from the early stages of throat cancer.

The retired general and former president often could be found bundled in blankets on the porch of his house at Mount McGregor, scribbling away at his memoirs.

Setting to Work

Immediately, he set about looking after the financial security of his family.

Earlier that year, the editor of *Century Magazine* had approached Grant about writing a series of essays on his Civil War campaigns. Grant reluctantly agreed and produced accounts of the battles of Shiloh and Vicksburg. The articles were so successful that *Century* asked Grant to consider writing his memoirs. "Do you really think," Grant asked, "anyone would be interested in a book by me?"

Despite pain and fatigue,

Grant worked every day. He sat at a large, square table in his study on the second floor of his New York home, interrupted only by his doctors and visits from his children and grandchildren.

Friendly Help

When Grant's friend Samuel Clemens (better known as Mark Twain) learned that Grant was writing a book, he also found out that *Century* was not paying Grant any advance money. Clemens, who had met Grant five years earlier at a dinner in Chicago, believed that the magazine probably would not pay Grant very well for his work either. So he called on Grant at his home.

Samuel Clemens, more popularly known as Mark Twain, encouraged Grant to write his memoirs.

After two days of hard negotiations, Clemens offered Grant a $10,000 advance and 70 percent of the book's net profits. Clemens's own publishing firm, Charles L. Webster & Company, would publish the book.

A Final Journey

By June 1885, Grant's condition was worse. The family decided to spend the summer at Mount McGregor, in the Adirondack Mountains of upstate New York. As their train rolled through the Hudson Valley, crowds gathered to cheer the great general on what would be his final journey.

Upon arriving at Mount McGregor, Grant set to work. When he was not writing, he received visitors and well-wishers, many of them former Union and Confederate officers. Despite these distractions, Grant kept writing, often sitting on the porch bundled in a blanket or settled in a chair in the house, pencil in hand, scribbling

This was one of the last photos taken of Ulysses S. Grant before his death on July 23, 1885.

furiously. He wrote that he was grateful "to witness these things," having lived long enough to see former enemies become friends.

Nothing More to Do

Meanwhile, Clemens sent an army of salesmen throughout the country to sell subscriptions to the book. The publisher was working around the clock to make sure the book would be ready on time. Delays arose in part from Grant's insistence on revising the manuscript himself. He wanted his book to be perfect.

Finally, on July 16, 1885, Grant laid down his pencil. "There is nothing more I should do to it now," he said. A week later, on July 23, 1885, he died.

Personal Memoirs of U.S. Grant proved to be a great critical and commercial success, selling more than 300,000 copies. The two-volume work was proudly displayed in many American parlors, evidence of Grant's enormous popularity.

The book's success also ensured his family's financial security. Clemens presented Julia Grant with the largest royalty check ever written at the time — $200,000. In the years to come, Grant's memoirs earned between $420,000 and $450,000 for his family.

With its clear, direct prose, *Personal Memoirs of U.S. Grant* remains one of the greatest military narratives ever written. Every page of this Civil War classic reflects the quiet dignity of its author.

A Final Resting Place

Richard Theodore Greener distinguished himself in many ways. He was the first African American graduate of Harvard University, in 1870. He earned a law degree while he was a professor and librarian at the

Grant's Tomb is an enormous granite and marble structure overlooking the Hudson River in New York City.

41

University of South Carolina. When the university excluded African Americans at the end of Reconstruction, Greener went to Howard University and became dean of the law school. One of Greener's proudest accomplishments, however, was raising funds to build the magnificent mausoleum known as "Grant's Tomb."

Idolizing Grant

Greener had been a senior in high school when the Civil War ended. He and his classmates had idolized Grant. They had adopted a motto, "I shall find a way, or make one," from the example Grant had set.

At one point, Grant and his wife had expressed their interest in being buried in New York. Upon Grant's death in 1885, the mayor of New York wired Julia Grant, extending an invitation to bury her husband there. She accepted. Greener was appointed secretary of the Grant Monument Association, which he regarded as a great personal honor. He believed that "like Washington and Lincoln, Grant was risen up by God to lead the Nation in a time of need."

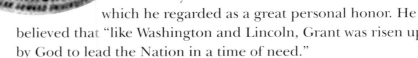

Richard T. Greener's efforts to raise money for the memorial to his hero paid off — more than $600,000 were donated and put toward the tomb's construction.

Raising Donations

Instructed to bring in private donations, Greener was instrumental in involving individuals and organizations all over New York City to help build the monument. Donation boxes were placed in elevated train stations, and riders contributed nickels and pennies.

Churches and community groups encouraged their members to participate. African Americans were especially responsive because of Grant's role in bringing an end to slavery. Philanthropists Cornelius Vanderbilt and J.P. Morgan were on the executive committee of the Grant Monument Association. Greener and General Horace Porter, a member of Grant's staff during the war, gave speeches to help raise money.

High Above the Hudson

After the association raised more than $600,000, an imposing white granite structure in Riverside Park was built high above the Hudson River. Both Ulysses and Julia Grant are entombed there. A display at the memorial tells of Greener's role in making it possible.

Since 1959, the memorial has been operated by the National Park Service. By 1994, however, the condition of the building and grounds had deteriorated. Grant's descendants considered moving the Grants' bodies to Galena, Illinois, where the Grants had lived before the Civil War. The state of Illinois even threatened to remove the Grants' bodies if the federal government and the state of New York did not restore the site.

The exterior of the building has since been cleaned up, and the interior renovated. The site was rededicated on April 27, 1997, in time to celebrate the tomb's centennial.

When Grant's Tomb was dedicated on April 27, 1897, more than 1 million people attended the ceremony.

CIVIL WAR

1860

NOV 6
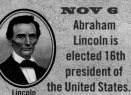

Lincoln

Abraham Lincoln is elected 16th president of the United States.

1861

FEB 9
Formation of the Confederate States of America (CSA) by secessionist states South Carolina, Mississippi, Florida, Alabama, Georgia, Louisiana, and Texas. Jefferson Davis elected CSA president.

Davis

MAR 4
Lincoln's inauguration

APR 12

Fort Sumter
(South Carolina) Civil War begins with Confederate attack under Gen. Pierre Beauregard.

APR 15
Lincoln issues proclamation calling

for 75,000 troops. Gen. Winfield Scott becomes commander of Union army.

APR 17
Virginia joins CSA, followed by Arkansas, Tennessee, and North Carolina.

APR 20
Gen. Robert E. Lee resigns from U.S. Army and accepts command in Confederate army.

JUL 21
First Manassas
(Virginia) Gen. Thomas J. "Stonewall" Jackson defeats Gen. Irvin McDowell.

NOV 1
Gen. George B. McClellan assumes command of Union forces.

1862

FEB 11-16
Fort Donelson (Tennessee) Gen. Ulysses S. Grant breaks major Confederate stronghold.

MAR
McClellan begins Peninsular Campaign, heading to Richmond,

Virginia, the Confederate capital.

APR 6-7
Shiloh (Tennessee) Grant defeats Beauregard and Gen. A.S. Johnston. Heavy losses on both sides.

APR 24

New Orleans (Louisiana) Gen. David Farragut leads 17 Union gunboats up Mississippi River and takes New Orleans, the South's most important seaport.

JUN 25-JUL 1
Seven Days (Virginia) Six major battles are fought over seven days near Richmond, Virginia. Lee is victorious, protecting the Confederate capital from Union occupation.

Halleck

JUL 18
Lincoln turns over command to Gen. Henry W. Halleck.

AUG 29-30
Second Manassas (Virginia) Jackson and Gen. James Longstreet defeat Gen. John Pope.

SEP 17
Antietam (Maryland) McClellan narrowly defeats Lee. Bloodiest day in American military history: 23,000 casualties.

SEP 22

Lincoln issues preliminary Emancipation Proclamation, freeing slaves in Confederate states.

OCT 3-4
Corinth (Mississippi) Gen. William Rosecrans defeats Gen. Earl Van Dorn.

NOTE: Battles are in black type, with flags indicating: Union victory 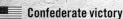 Confederate victory

TIME LINE

NOV 7
Lincoln replaces McClellan with Gen. Ambrose Burnside to lead Army of the Potomac.

Burnside

DEC 13
Fredericksburg
(Virginia)
Lee defeats Burnside.

1863

JAN 1
Final Emancipation Proclamation frees slaves in Confederate states. Union army begins enlisting black soldiers.

JAN 25
Lincoln replaces Burnside with Gen. Joseph Hooker.

Hooker

JAN 29
Grant is placed in command of the Union army in the West.

MAY 1-4
Chancellorsville
(Virginia)
Lee defeats Hooker.

JUN 28
Lincoln replaces Hooker with Gen. George E. Meade.

JUL 1-3

Gettysburg
(Pennsylvania)
Meade defeats Lee.

JUL 4
Vicksburg
(Mississippi)
After weeks of seige, Grant takes the Confederate stronghold on Mississippi River, effectively dividing eastern and western Confederate forces.

SEP 18-20
Chickamauga (Georgia)
Gen. Braxton Bragg defeats Rosecrans.

OCT 16
Lincoln puts Grant in charge of all western operations.

NOV 19
Lincoln delivers the Gettysburg Address, dedicating the battlefield as a national cemetery.

NOV 23-25
Chattanooga (Tennessee)
Grant defeats Bragg.

1864

MAR 9
Lincoln puts Grant in command of entire Union army. Gen. William T. Sherman takes over western operations.

MAY 8-21
Spotsylvania
(Virginia)
Grant defeats Lee.

MAY 31-JUN 12
Cold Harbor (Virginia)
Lee defeats Grant and Meade.

JUN 15-18

Petersburg (Virginia)
Lee and Beauregard defeat Grant and Meade.

NOV 8
Lincoln is re-elected.

NOV 15-DEC 21

Sherman's "March to the Sea." Sherman destroys supplies and transportation systems from Atlanta to Savannah (Georgia), crippling the Confederacy.

1865

APR 2
Petersburg (Virginia)
Grant defeats Lee. Confederates leave Richmond.

APR 9
Lee surrenders to Grant at Appomattox Court House, Virginia.

APR 14
Lincoln is shot by John Wilkes Booth at Ford's Theatre, Washington, D.C. He dies the following morning.

DEC 6
Thirteenth Amendment to the Constitution abolishing slavery is ratified.

Lee

GRAPHICS BY FRED CARLSON

Glossary

Adjutant: In the military, an officer who helps a commander with administrative affairs.

Adversaries: Enemies or opponents.

Ammunition: Anything that can be thrown or shot — such as a bullet, rock, or cannonball — for use to attack or defense.

Artillery: Soldiers who specialize in the use of heavy weapons, such as cannon.

Battery: Placement of artillery (soldiers and weapons).

Cadet: A student at a military school training to become an officer.

Campaign: In military terms, a series of battles, or other operations, in a particular area to accomplish a specific goal.

Casualties: In war, the victims: the injured, killed, captured, or missing in action.

Cavalry: Soldiers who fight on horseback.

Civil war: A war fought between people of the same nation.

Civilian: A person who is not an active member of the military or police.

Commission: An official government document that bestows powers and rank on someone in the military.

Confederacy: In the American Civil War, the alliance of states that broke ties with the U.S. government to form a new government, called the Confederate States of America. The states that did not secede supported the Union.

Confederate: A supporter of the American Confederacy, which was an alliance of states that broke ties with the U.S. government.

Corps: In the military, a separate combat division with a special assignment.

Correspondent: A person who works for a newspaper or other broadcast company, supplying news on a regular basis. *Correspondence* refers to letters written and received.

Demerits: Marks made against a school record.

Dysentery: An intestinal ailment, usually caused by a parasite, causing severe abdominal pain, fever, and diarrhea.

Earthworks: Mounds of earth erected as protective fortifications.

Flank: Right or left side of a military formation.

Flotilla: Smaller division of a naval fleet, consisting of two or more groups of boats.

Infantry: Soldiers who fight on foot.

Ironclads: Warships having sides armored with metal plates.

Mausoleum: A large stately tomb or a building that contains one or more tombs.

Mortar shells: Bombs fired from cannon at short ranges that explode when they hit a target.

Offensive: In war, an attack or assault.

Philanthropists: People who promote human welfare through charitable aid or donations.

Reconstruction: Period following the Civil War (1865–1877) when the federal government concentrated on rebuilding the war-torn nation.

Regiment: A military unit of ground troops. *Regimental* refers to something orderly and strict.

Siege: Attempt to capture a place by surrounding it and battering it until it surrenders.

Skirmish: A small conflict between enemies that can often lead to a larger battle.

Tannery: Place where animal hides are converted into leather.

Union: In the American Civil War, the states that supported the United States government. The states that did not support the U.S. seceded to form the Confederate States of America.

Veteran: Person who served in the armed forces.

Index

COBBLESTONE®
The CIVIL WAR Series

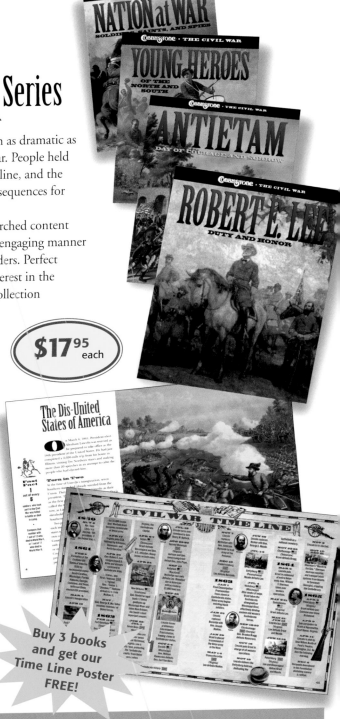

Few events in our nation's history have been as dramatic as those leading up to and during the Civil War. People held strong views on each side of the Mason-Dixon line, and the clash of North and South had far-reaching consequences for our country that are still being felt today.

Each 48-page book delivers the solidly researched content *COBBLESTONE®* is known for, written in an engaging manner that is sure to retain the attention of young readers. Perfect for report research or pursuing an emerging interest in the Civil War, these resources will complete your collection of materials on this important topic.

$17⁹⁵ each

Each sturdy, hardcover volume includes:
- Fair and balanced depictions of people and events
- Well-researched text ■ Historical photographs
- Glossary ■ Time line

NATION AT WAR: SOLDIERS, SAINTS, AND SPIES	COB67900
YOUNG HEROES OF THE NORTH AND SOUTH	COB67901
ABRAHAM LINCOLN: DEFENDER OF THE UNION	COB67902
GETTYSBURG: BOLD BATTLE IN THE NORTH	COB67903
ANTIETAM: DAY OF COURAGE AND SACRIFICE	COB67904
ROBERT E. LEE: DUTY AND HONOR	COB67905
ULYSSES S. GRANT: CONFIDENT LEADER AND HERO	COB67906
STONEWALL JACKSON: SPIRIT OF THE SOUTH	COB67907
JEFFERSON DAVIS AND THE CONFEDERACY	COB67908
REBUILDING A NATION: PICKING UP THE PIECES	COB67909

Buy 3 books and get our Time Line Poster FREE!